2006

One Hundred Steps from Shore

One Hundred Steps from Shore

Jenifer Browne Lawrence

Jenifer Browne Lawrence

Blue Begonia Press Yakima, WA

Blue Begonia Press
225 S. 15th Ave.
Yakima, WA 98902
(509) 452-9748
bluebegoniapress.com

Library of Congress Cataloging-in-Publication Data

Lawrence, Jenifer Browne, 1958-
  One hundred steps from shore / Jenifer Browne Lawrence.
    p. cm.
  Poems.
  ISBN-13: 978-0-911287-56-1 (pbk. : alk. paper)
  ISBN-10: 0-911287-56-6 (pbk. : alk. paper)
  I. Title.

PS3612.A947O54 2006
811'.6—dc22
                        2006016390

In memory of Carolyn Browne and Roger W. Browne, Jr.

For Linda, Roger, Hilary and Georgia

We have many stories to tell. This is one of them. I know your stories are different than what is written here. A child fills in the gaps where knowledge is lacking. What is given is small, and much remains to be told.

Contents

Learning to Paint

Tales from the 20th Century

Snow Elegy

ONE HUNDRED STEPS FROM SHORE
St. Ann's Hospital, Juneau, Alaska, August 13, 1971

My sister dumps a puzzle on the table.
We don't follow the usual rule
of not looking at the picture on the box.
Wheat bends toward the red siding of a farmhouse.
The barn is bigger than the house.
Paint peels off its long boards.
A row of poplars edges the lawn
and a thicket of trees stands behind the field.

We work the puzzle, find the edges first.
We form the frame before we begin the middle.
Mom and Dad go in and out of the waiting room.
They bring paper bowls of chocolate pudding
and little wooden paddles.

The bathroom door is heavy.
When I come out a policeman waits.
We sit on the orange couch.
Someone has drawn a daisy on it.
He asks me my name, how old I am,
asks me what I saw, how I knew.
He asks me about the pickup, where it was
on the road, where my sister was,
what I saw, what I heard.
He asks what the driver said,
a small man with white hair,
asks what he said and I tell him.
He said he honked, he said she jumped in front of him.
He said he honked to warn her not to cross,
and she jumped in front of him.

The policeman asks what I saw, what I heard.
He wants to know if I heard a screech.
I tell him no, just a thud, and I ran to see
and I saw her. He asks me what I saw,

what I heard. I tell him I smelled pennies.
I tell him I saw her and she was fine, lying there,
hair in her eyes and a puddle beneath her head.

The policeman has an unlined notebook
and a pencil like the one I use in school.
He writes everything down, he asks me again.
He asks what I did then and I tell him.
I tell him my mother is running up the steps.
I see my mother and try to stop her,
I put my arms in front of her, tell her not to look.
She says *Let me see* and I tell her *It's Carolyn*. I tell her
it's Carolyn and that she is hit.
He asks me what then and I tell him
and he asks me what then
and I tell him.

We go back to the puzzle and we finish the house.
We build the barn and the poplar trees.
My older sister works on the wheat.
My younger sister works on the sky.
My mother sits with a puzzle piece in her hand
and peels the picture from the cardboard.
My father brings us more pudding.
He lies down on the couch and doesn't close his eyes.
We work on the puzzle and the field is full of wheat.
We start on the birch grove, the snow-white trunks.
We build the trees from the green down to wheat
and there is nothing left but sky.

We are holding pieces in our hands
and the waiting room door swings open.
The doctor is there in the doorway.
He stands there and puts his left palm on its window.
He stands on the threshold and doesn't come in.
His clothes are wrinkled, they are green as the walls.
His hair is silver and sticks to his forehead.
He sees us watching and he watches us back.

He looks at the pieces of sky in our hands
and he looks at our faces one by one.
He looks at our hands and he looks at our eyes
and he looks at my mother and no one says anything.
He takes a deep breath and says nothing.
He takes a deep breath and shakes his head.
He shakes his head from side to side
and his hair falls into his eyes.

My brother rescued two mallards
from the tide flats where their feet
had frozen to the icy muck.
He'd watched them flap their wings
against the tide, had raced
to meet them, carried one under each arm,
the same birds he and my father
hunted in the fall. We kept them
in the bathtub for a week, took sponge baths
while the ducks watched, dying,
and we buried them in the woods,
digging beneath February snow.

After her funeral, nobody spoke my sister's name.
We took our cue from Mom and Dad, pretending
she had never lived. Until the door fell open
and they stood wordless, explaining finally
that a dog was dead on the road, and they
had come home because to them
It wasn't a dog.

I was six when my father's mother died,
my image of her all lap and rocking chair—
so when they told me, I whispered
But I don't want her to die and Mom said
I don't either and pulled me into her lap.
That was the talk we had about death.
Maybe, when Carolyn died, everything
had already been said.

We continued trying to save injured birds,
orphaned squirrels, any life
small enough to carry, and they continued
dying. A raven with a broken wing
was taped and housed, fed bits of raw ground beef.
For weeks it lived in a cardboard box,
terrible and wounded.

And then the raven picked the tape away,
plucked at its feathers and raised its wings.
It flew up and down the hallway,
window to window, shitting.
We opened the door
and it went squawking into the firs.
For the rest of our time together
we relived this one success,
this life winging away
without looking back.

HARBINGER

When she was five and I was four
my sister skipped
between manzanita and redwood,

kicked a nest
of yellow jackets.
Her playmates passed

on either side of the trees,
turned to hysteria in a stinging
cloud. Her face was

swarmed away, I saw
through my tears the wasps
had killed her, the boy and girl

holding on to her hands
pulled a headless body
from the wash of autumn woods.

Rooted

A tire swing hangs from the lowest branch.
Children take turns, grab an outstretched foot

and spin until the rider throws up or falls out.
The middle child climbs the tree. She sprawls

along an upper limb and watches through the leaves.
She sees the rope, the tire, the sister clinging tight.

She sees the dance of dust beneath the swing,
the whirl of head and feet, her sister's eyes

brown bullets, and knows herself the focus,
the anchor fixed to keep the dizziness at bay.

Maybe we were making angels
in the yard. A stationwagon swerved,
plowed you under. The neighbor's cat
crossed the road. A white helicopter
took you. It was the first
Christmas since we moved

from Santa Cruz to Valdez.
The neighbor stayed, kissed us
goodnight, her breath like Daddy's
after supper. We took down the tree,
no one to tell us which box
each ornament came from.

We walked around the ice
to catch the school bus,
to come home. The stain
seeped all the way to asphalt,
all the way to hibernating
iris in the yard. Each snowfall

brought the plow, its blade
uncovering your blood. You relearned
our names, the cupboard where we kept
the toys. You were younger, different.
We bought you a cat of your own,
black as your new-grown hair.

MAKING OUT
North Douglas Road, 1971

My sister's breast puckers under a boy's touch
and she wants him to stop, wants me to make him.
She rubs her thighs flat-palmed, a sign
recognized but not acknowledged. Absorbed

in the reaction of my boyfriend, I am
pushing my body against his, the power
I wield, the boy a spaniel whimpering
at my kindness. Younger by fifteen months,

I am still her older sister. I do not tell her
to move the boy's hand from her breast.
Instead I make the motion she is making
with her palms, and shake my head

so that she stops. The one that's kissing her
is the boy with black magnets for eyes, lashes
that curl from his lids the way we try to curl ours
with tiny tongs in front of the mirror.

Neither of us knows anything
about standing our ground. At our house,
the practice is to do whatever it takes,
less *turn your cheek* than

close your eyes and pretend.
The lesson has been passed through
generations like a relay baton:
We do not save each other.

Because the dress I wanted was not in the closet,
my mother spoke: *They told me*
to find something for her to wear.
I gave them the blue shoes, too.
It is supposed to rain when someone dies,
but it was hot at the cemetery.
The McNabb boys were there, and the Caldwells.
They lived on either side of us,
about a half-mile between each house.
My brother, gone two weeks at the academy
in New London when she died,
did not come home.
I don't remember why she was taking a walk.
Seven of us lived in a one-bedroom house,
we spent a lot of time outside.
I stole a dollar once, from her savings, a roll of bills
held together with rubber bands in her drawer.
She counted and counted—23, 24, 25.
I had 26 dollars. You took one.
She sat on the edge of the bed,
rubbing her hands fast on her thighs,
the way she did when she was upset
and didn't know what else to do.

Ten years after my sister's death, my husband ran over a two-year-
old boy. I was in Juneau visiting family when he called. *I told her not*
to pick him up, but she did. He let go of his sister's hand. He was
shorter than the truck and I didn't see him. They were waiting for the
light. The light turned green and I went. It almost tore his ear off, a
lot of blood, filled his sister's lap where they sat on the curb. I asked
how the boy was now, how he was. He did not know the answer to
either, said the policeman recommended he not call the hospital, not
apologize because that would be admitting guilt. *But how can I not?*

I spent eighth grade at the cemetery, tossing french-fries to crows,
eating sandwiches from the hamburger stand next to the junior high.
The school was right across the street from the graveyard.
I didn't visit her, sat instead under a Douglas fir and talked to birds,
coaxed them close with fried potatoes. By spring, one of the crows
would take a french fry from my hand, hop backward before swallowing.

Our house sits on a shoreline
at the bottom of a steep bank,
a hundred steps to the front door.
The stairs wind around trees, over small ravines
of devil's club and salmonberry.
There are stretches of boardwalk between steps,
pillared above the damp soil.
We cart every grocery bag down, every trash bag up, week after week.
We can take the stairs down in about twelve seconds.
The trip up is twenty-five at a dead run.

On my brother's eighteenth birthday, in his absence, there is no cake.
I am outside on the wrap-around deck.
At ten, my father paid me a dollar an hour to paint it,
2x4's covered with a redwood stain.
I hear something but I don't know what.
I yell through the door that I am going to the road.
I run up the steps, faster even than when my brother dares me to race him.
The stairs end in a parking area filled flat above the slope to the water.
Salmonberry grows higher than my head,
and I have to round the corner of the bushes to see.

A girl is lying on the pavement.
She could be asleep except for the pool
widening under her hair.
A man is standing in the road.
The centerline gleams beneath his boots.
He looks from her to me.
I look at the girl.
She wears a green sweatshirt
like one I have. No. It is my shirt,
the Snoopy sweatshirt that says

Born to Sleep in the Sun
and the sun is shining on the blood,
blinding me with its light.

TURNING
Sol Duc River, Olympic National Park

The sun's tears—maybe
I made that up,
but the moving water spits

its language in my path.
Three o'clock and Douglas fir
shadows moss-colored stones,

covered stones nudging
from under the Sol Duc, slick
shoulders against the current.

Leaning into the spray
I sweep boulders with my eyes,
learn their crevices early

in June. Flushing in the wash
of river, bits of deer moss
shred on the beaten banks

but it's the devil's club
cupping its huge hands on the far side
that I love most, waving

farewell to the sun, steadfast
as I am not.

ON THE ANNIVERSARY OF YOUR DEATH

Rain in windless air shines the deck rail flat,
a rink upon which raindrops skate, land fat
and singular, splash from the rail in
a dozen tiny pearls as though leaping
to form a crown for one behind the glass,
spill back, broken strand across the wood, beads
washing lengthwise until they slip over,
reconnect, drip to the ground,
where I cannot see to tell
if jewels or oceans enter the grass.

PORCUPINE CHILD

wounded at roadside
pricking my skin as we hurry
toward the hope of more capable hands

the fog line a blur beneath tears
and torn sneakers the same line
crossed when my sister fell to the pickup

cars come up fast as the tides
the quilled baby hammocked
in my shirt mews and mews

how did I come to be
the ferryman burying over
and over the same stick in the water

taking babies across
the black river rubbing
their stains into my belly

SWEEPING THE SKY

DECOYS

Two days before hunting season my father melts lead
in an iron pot while we dig holes in the yard
with teaspoons from the kitchen drawer.
He stirs with a green branch until the kettle shakes.
At any moment a finger will disappear in it,

come out bone, or nothing at all. Steam rises
into his nostrils with cigarette smoke until
he becomes Merlin, waving a silver wand
over holes and beer cans and children.
My brother follows behind the ladle,

inserts wire into scalded holes, balances
looped ends until they burn him. When the yard
is pocked with lead we traipse inside
trailing dirt and bent spoons. Mother tries
to look disapproving but she forgives

anything. The handles are still hot, the holes
like rows of dollhouse teacups, but we pull anyway,
toss the weights in water that hisses
at each intrusion. We carry decoys from the shed,
lay them at my father's feet. He spent all summer

cradling the birds, touching them with his paintbrush.
Underneath, rubber loops prevent the ducks
from sitting upright anywhere but water.
We twist more wire to anchor weight to bird,
one for teal, two for mallard. We line them up,

their painted eyes staring, the kettle
glazed with lead, my father coughing,
a Pall Mall hanging from his lip.
Opening Day. Only he and my brother go,
and it is thirty years before

I learn what happened there—my father
with too much brandy and my brother
tired and cold, the shotguns pointed
at each other instead of the sky, ducks flying over
unharmed, decoys motionless on the pond.

I remember waiting for the salmon run in June,
the patient oiling, rewinding of our reels, stress
kept on the filament for evenness, half-moon
nickel key wedged in the fishhold ring, how we'd obsess
to reach Bird Rock before high tide, floating snake
of pollen and debris a current rendered moot
on days the Coho followed herring to the black cake
of glacier rock, that sheer face we called Old Beaut
for its power to lure the silvers in, how Garbo,
our Chocolate Lab, shivered on point until we'd play
a salmon out, then vault over the side like a hobo
leaping from a freight car, her tail wagging all day
for a single landed fish, its scaled rhinestone
sloughed across the deck in slick, salt-washed cologne.

YOU CAN SMELL THE RAIN COMING

a long way off
first it brings down
dirt and exhaust

eyes that burned all summer
in fierce pollen close
in the lowering air

this morning
the dew is finer
than yesterday

the telephone relays
details of a sister's
passing

on the tight-knot cedar
windowsill another fly
spins on its back

the first drops slant
against the pane still
a long way off

REPLACING THE DECK

With my brother, work is acceptable
discussion: the pry bar demolition
of rotting wood, mitered deck ends
nailed down, circular saw whirring
as we cover, one board at a time,
the rain-grooved soil beneath the deck,
dirt strewn with matchbox cars
and crayons, the empty can of insecticide
that only stirred the wasps to anger.

Not speaking of taking our lives
by the napes and dragging them
back in the house. Dark, his eyes
spark memories that crack
like the chocolate coating
on soft-dip cones we mouthed
on trips to town—how the hard shell
flaked off, where vanilla pushed out
dripping, how it had to be licked at once,
before any of it touched our skin.

When the cardiologist says her father
is not a candidate for transplant
she lies in the grass, squints at a fissure
in the sidewalk. Pill bugs cross
each other's paths. Shepherd's Purse
scatters triangular shade. A carpenter ant
turns to light, marches from the crack. It bends
a green blade and never looks back.
But there is solace in the unlit rift
and she crawls in, joins segmented,
gray-shelled inhabitants, curls
into a ball at each dangerous vibration.
She is less resolute than the ant,
less effusive than the white-capped weeds
stretching sunward to offer unblemished
two-sided hearts to any passing stranger.

She Stamps Her Feet

to warn the garter snakes
before she starts the mower,

rehearses the accuracy of medication
doled out to her husband today.

Her needs set aside five decades,
more if you count the years

she ran the house for Pop
while her mother served in the war.

She kneads the bread dough without complaint,
accepting her arthritic thumbs,

the cemented arteries of her husband.
She measures systolic and diastolic,

body weight and blood sugar,
dispenses insulin and Lasix,

potassium, nitroglycerin, tolerates
the clear tubing that winds

through their days and down
the stairs into the bedroom.

But when the snake flies to pieces,
spatters her old Keds green and red,

she leaves the lawn untended,
snatches up the Pyrex bowl,

punches down the dough, nine years old
again, in the kitchen, eyes on the doorway

where her uniformed mother stands,
a last reminder about duty.

VIGILS

The field mouse lay on the garage floor
like a dropped rag.

We huddled close to see if the mouse was dead
or only playing, bowed our heads in the dim light,

our hair hanging in a circle above our shoes.
The mouse gathered its legs beneath it, closed its eyes.

The scent of oil and gasoline rose from my father's motorcycle
where it rested on upended milk crates, so that years later,

gathered around his hospital bed behind pink and brown curtains
this is what I smell, this memory of mouse and oil,

that long vigil until exhaustion and daylight
overtook us, and we nodded at the suggestion.

MY FATHER'S NURSE
Harrison Memorial Hospital, November 29, 2001

Now she hands me a slim gold band,
a drawstring bag of belongings.
I slip the still-warm ring on my thumb,
peer into the bag, discover
a blonde wig. I show it to Rhonda,
shake my head. She raises an eyebrow
at our common thought,
flings back the cotton drape
surrounding the bed. There he is,
still dead, white wisps of hair
stirring in the curtain's wake.

Belly to palm—he taught me to hold the herring. Run the double
leader through the sockets. Hooks catch and refuse to let go
of the eyes. Inside loop over the head to snub shut the mouth.
Wrap the dorsal fin. Anchor the upper hook in the ribs, the lower
just above the tail. Place a thumbnail at the shaft, pull without
tearing flesh, snug out the slack. Lean over the transom to rinse off
the scales. Slide the herring in to check its action—stutter of a
wounded fish in a forest of still water on the lee shore of Marmion,
trolling in the Whaler with a four-horse Johnson, barely moving
in the slack tide. Keep a thumb on the drag. Strip line from the reel.
Count out the depth for Kings.

SWEEPING THE SKY

She smoothes embroidered sofa pillows
the way she soothed wrinkles from his forehead
those nights in ICU. We speak of finding a home
for the dog, of selling and moving on.
She nods at her own words.

Her kiss unwrinkles his brow a moment,
the only sound the respirator's hiss. The oxymeter
turns his finger translucent red, the monitor blinks
its green heart, pulsing next to an uneven progression of line.
We watch his signs fluctuate, our hearts rise and fall.

I haven't told her Dad's last words,
Where's your mother? Nor how, as though it were
the truth, I told him he would see her in the morning,
that she'd gone home before it got too dark to see.
He turned his face to keep me from seeing.

I want to tell you of that first fishing trip
when he put me in an open boat, off the coast
of Santa Cruz, pitching in the swell of the Pacific,
the image of an orange sun when I was four,
the lost buoyancy when the lead broke water,
salmon pole wedged between my thighs, the sudden drown
of weight against me. I want to tell you how his brown hand
reached across the transom and cupped the heavy painted ball,
how he took the weight, let it thud between my feet and how the wind
in his dark hair lifted strands like waves and set them down again.

She stands at his side, watching,
although there is nothing to see.
He is not conscious, but his face
is full of tension and we seek relief,
stare at Monets on the wall outside his room.

The nurse increases a morphine drip, forces breath
into his lungs as he lies there taped and catheterized,

this act of dying completely without privacy.
Those words he spoke, *Where's your mother?*
When he knew, when he has always known.

I want to tell you about that autumn in Valdez
when the crowberries ripened and fireweed burned
on the hills. How he took my mother on a moose hunt,
and when they chanced upon a bull in a clearing he urged her
to take the shot. She hit the animal in the antler.
It bellowed a retreat. My father laughed
harder each time he told the story
of how the moose escaped.

Is he likely to wake?
The doctor has just showered.
Damp hair curls around his collar.
No. We can wake him if you want.
It won't be pleasant, but we can pull the morphine,
give him some dopamine, a few minutes.

Mom shakes her head, resigned
to a silent goodbye, the one
she has been saying for three years.
He asks if we would like to be present
when they remove the respirator.
Not if he isn't going to wake up.

I want to tell you of the sound of the chainsaw
on that lot out North Douglas,
of the rush of air before the ground
trembled at the falling, how his voice calling *Timber*
was drowned by branches sweeping through the forest.
How he lifted thin slices of yellow cedar, ringed plates
for us to break into pieces and put back together
on top of a stump while he worked.
How he handed the ax to each of us in turn,
to try our hand at splitting a chunk of green log,
and turned his half-smile from us.

I want to tell you how his hands at forty trembled
holding a red thermos lid of tea, of the steam
rising to his nostrils as he bent to sip.
I want to tell you how we ran around
with upraised branches, sweeping the sky
and shouting to Steller's jay and raven
in the midst of the clearing, how we were all
living and dying at the same time, without sorrow.

LEARNING TO PAINT

Our five-year-old bodies
in a bed of long needles
off the edge of the path
between our homes,
shimmy from clothes,
kneel to compare
our differences. White
in the dapple of pine,
our torsos, like candles
at an altar before marriage
gleam until crossed
by the shadow of god
come to call us to supper.

THE RESERVOIR
Valdez, 1966

My brother and I dragged sticks along its circumference, rubbed
our hands into its rusted curves and chased up and down the
beach, threatening to turn each other orange. We found an opening
at the base where a welded seam had split. Outside was summer,
but inside—the end of November. Diesel residue gagged us as we
stood, trying to see through darkness. I knew better than to ask
him to hold my hand.

Opposite the hole, a ladder ran to the top, a square hint of sky
lighting its rails. Working our way around, we shivered and
shouted *hello* until my brother threw *shit* across the emptiness, and
shit came floating back. We dragged our palms along the wall,
made it to the ladder. He climbed. I cried. He said *shut up* and
jumped from a rung higher than my head.

He crossed the circle, wiggled through the seam. The bright hole
disappeared. I scraped along the metal arc, knees chafing on the
gritty floor. I reached something soft and pushed, landed outside
on my brother's jacket. I sucked in clean air, sat there, blinking at
the blood, the oily rust coating my hands and knees.

He stood at the shore, skipped rocks across the water. I ran, shoved
him hard as I could. He didn't lose his balance, didn't even turn
around to say it: *Baby.*

A Cottonwood Leaf Can Be Taken Apart

so gently it does not bleed, though its essence
lodges in the heart like an eight-year-old
in the arms of a tree.

i.

Fireweed burns up the hillside in a slant of morning sun.
It is late summer on the Richardson Highway,
midway between Glenallen and Valdez.
Yesterday's inner tube floats on the pond.

She searches for the beaver that swims
with branches in tow. She will swim with her brother
and sisters every day until the end of summer
when they return to town for school and pending snows.

In early August cottonwood discard green
and take on the womanly scent of blood and balsam.
The odor clings to her clothes
when she slides down a leaf-coated slope.

She smells like her mother does on Sundays,
doesn't understand why that is, only knows
what her sister tells her: *When Mom smells like that*
in the morning, it's because of the sex.

She gathers leaves in her arms, tosses them up
and turns her face to catch as many as she can.
None of them land on her tongue yet their taste
brings saliva, and she swallows and closes her eyes.

At eight, she knows only that her desire to lie down
and roll in the leaves is as strong as any she's known,
that the biggest cottonwood in this stand is the hide-and-seek
home base and that—for now—her brother will win every game.

ii.

She breathes out all the way, then sucks in
hard and fast to flatten a green leaf
against her nostrils, to make a vacuum there
beneath the cottonwood and try to live in it.

Once, she thought she was going to do it,
hold her breath exactly forever,
but she woke with a leaf on her chest,
dizzy and missing her mom.

iii.

Because she has nothing else to do until supper,
because her brother went fishing without her,
she strips a leaf, one chamber at a time,
exposing capillaries that branch from the leafstalk.

Thumbs and fingers come together on either side
as though she is miming binoculars. She pinches
and the leaf decides where to open.
She continues until the leaf is tattered,

hanging by a thread to its spine.
A shredded mountain in her palm,
she stretches and rolls down the hill,
arms above her head. She rolls

until buds embed sap in her skin. She rolls,
and twigs poke her torso and thighs.
She rolls over and over, gathering
dirt and leaves and the scent of cottonwood.

LEARNING TO PAINT
Eagle Creek Trailer Court, 1968

It was the time we found all those cans in an empty house and transformed a stranger's floor into a work of art. We pried open gallons of bathroom pink and kitchen green, swirled patterns with curtain rods plucked from the windows, skied across wet canvas. We tossed our shoes in someone else's trash, sneaked through our own back door.

We ran a hot bath, climbed in both at once, shoved our paint-laden clothes in the washer. Scrubbing until our skin reddened, we lay back at either end of the tub, the toes of one even with the ears of the other and began to talk about boys.

Lying there in hot water with the washer agitating we wondered aloud how our first kiss might be. Lisa said we had to be ready or no one would ever kiss us. She said *like this* and I watched her lips pooch out and smack the soft skin of her left hand just above the crease of thumb. *Sit up. Pretend you're a boy.*

The air was steamy. I always did what Lisa said. Water sloshed over the edge and when I leaned to blot it she kissed me. She tipped her head and said *now you kiss me* and I did. *Again,* she said and we did, our lips learning to be ready.

We kissed there in the bathtub until the washing machine shuddered to a stop and we began to shiver. Lisa pulled the drain plug. We sat hugging our knees, watching water sluice past our haunches and through the arches of our feet.

We hold small rectangles of glass, microscopes bolted to a counter in front of us. One needle per row, the teacher hands them out. We swivel to watch Andrew, freckles the only color in his face. He could skip a grade but won't ask. He passes the needle to the new girl, Rebecca. They say she's being molested, but she shakes her head and smiles at any questions, the same expression now when Andrew jabs at her request.

Kelly kisses girls, poured Everclear in my soda at the movies once, and dared me. She stabs herself and then stabs me, draws blood, and I don't bother to prick my finger, but scrape the slide across my skin where she has opened it. She leans against me for the hand-off to Lorraine, who has a week of velvet chokers and big teeth. A hickey shows at the edge of Monday's ribbon. Lorraine pokes twice to find what's in her, and the needle moves to the end of the row.

Home Economics

Laura's split ends filter sunlight
onto my jeans. She sits sideways
at her desk, holding a photo
by one corner. She looks me

in the eye, says while she was sleeping
her dad took off his pajamas
and snapped away. Sometimes
she wakes up to find him on her bed.

She says once when she opened
her mouth he pushed in. She says
it was hot and salty, that it tasted
like battery acid feels, tingly, bitter.

She could be describing a soft pretzel,
or how she learned to tie her shoes.
She pins a paper sleeve to cloth,
turns her face to the sun.

A tracing wheel lies on Laura's desk.
I pick it up, run it back and forth
along my palm, pressing in,
making red indentations.

In the background, girls are giggling.
Small motors start and stutter.
A yard of pink material lies on the floor,
pattern fastened to it, blue text

directing: *Cut here. Sew along this line.*
Pins stick out in all directions
though the teacher said be careful
to point them all one way.

I push harder, trying to feel it,
to come as close as I dare

to bleeding. The sun is warm
on my shirt. I feel the fabric

strain against my chest. *No shit*, I say,
my hands cold, the wheel digging
a dotted line that I follow
all the way back to my desk.

Taillight remnants, beer cans—the roadside shoulder tends to hold
its own. But the underpants in the ditch curl around a hemlock
seedling, defiantly vivid.

> *An old Satellite rumbles by in darkness. Bodies in the back
> move together, while the driver and his date suck in ragged
> breaths and turn up the stereo. There's a smooth heel print on
> fogged glass. A toe coaxes lace down a thin calf, releases it to
> the breeze.*

The next week, and the next, the panties haven't budged.
All summer they challenge the salmonberry blossoms and wild
rose. In August a heavy rain bundles them up to drift toward
the estuary. It may have been the first time, rural conception,
signature on the back seat of a '71 Plymouth. That was June.
It's February. These panties won't fit her now.

> *She slaps her stomach hard as she dares. Nothing fits over her
> swollen belly. Her breasts strain at a stretch crop tank,
> bellybutton protruding, a dark stripe dividing her from the
> world. He's not coming back. She slips into the bath, only her
> abdomen unsubmerged.*

A mallard lies glued to the tide flats, emerald head twisted to the
sky. Saltwater surges and ebbs, rain collects to trickle or rage
through the gravel and algae of the ditch. The panties edge closer to
the outfall, perhaps five yards since summer.

> *She remembers the suction of his mouth on her throat and
> cannot catch her breath. When her water breaks, sea washes
> into the creek bed.*

KEEPING OUR HEADS UNDERWATER
Mendenhall Lake, Alaska, 1974

Woodsmoke sculpts our torsos
by firelight we rub sap
between finger and thumb
milkgreen floes
deaden our limbs
we are motionless
as the river we swim
under the glacier to see
what blue means the ice keeps
its secret we could burn
if the glacier would
calve if icebergs knew
which way to float
Mendenhall
you scoop red salmon
in blue nets your clouds
scrub pollen from the spruce
you wrap our shoulders
a blanket of mist
smoke rising
through flame ochered fir

EVERY LEAP YEAR DANCING

Shelly was always a year older, always
tugging wayward kinks at parties, she was
always the one who looked best in skintight
jeans we pegged by hand. Shelly hated her hair
almost as much as she hated her brother
for going to Vietnam, for sitting in a helicopter
riveting rice paddies and coarse-woven indigo,
hated the way her hair turned to wool when it rained
and it always rained in Juneau in 1972.

We drowned in music that punctured the air
like coiled wire, we peeled our clothes
to dance on grained tapestry tacked
to a pine floor in the loft of the last house
on River Street. Shelly haloed in lamplight dimmed
with a purple bedsheet, the Allman Brothers jamming
Pony Boy through our pores, the notes uncurling,
turning us until we collapsed, lying
so close my breath frayed through Shelly's hair.

AND WE ARE BOUND AWAY

Joel taught my sister to lead the grouse,
to shoot in front of its path so that the bird flew
into the buckshot, so that, he explained,
it wasn't really her doing the killing.
And she taught Joel how to pluck the grouse,
to hold his breath when the crop was cut,
the way we'd learned on ducks
Dad brought down with his shotgun.

When Joel joined Search and Rescue
he couldn't have known a 727
would slam into the mountain,
that there would be no rescue,
that he'd become a garbage man
maneuvering halves of bodies
into plastic bags, passengers sheared
by their safety belts, innards congealed
in the opened cavities of their bodies.

After that he kept one hand at his belt
when he traveled. In the air, on the ground,
it didn't matter, he said, he'd rather be tossed
through a windshield into a Sitka spruce,
launched into sea or mountainside,
than be cut in half, to be buried
or burned in pieces.
When my sister left him to follow God,
Joel followed me, sometimes called me

by her name. He practiced yoga
and massage, lifted my calves
in his palms, kneaded
the tension he found.
He quit driving, took his life
day by day, stepped in the path
of a Greyhound bus, one hand
gripping the buckle of his belt.

TALES FROM THE 20ᵀᴴ CENTURY

Looking into the Night, a Shooting Star Goes Unnoticed

We think we can't do without it, let slip
into place a substitution—desire or attention,
call it fire, stars—and the hard knot of being
condenses, becomes something near to coal,
near airless. As if a body could sieve itself
to fill another's empty spaces,
as if by allowing oneself to be taken
apart one could make, of another, a whole.
Instead, the armor of compression,
cold-pressing the knots, as if we could fill
the gravelly gaps in our own bodies, as if
just by wanting it, a star could set itself on fire.

Where did it go, the element that allowed her
to pluck a fallen popsicle from the sidewalk
and lick on the opposite side from the ants?
Ants traveling the flat stick at a loss—
how to gather sugar in this form,
feet cool and sticky, hard pebbles
of their heads turning from her mouth
to artificially flavored limbs, following
a lime-green drip down her wrist,
her knee, back to hot concrete,
forgoing intangible sweetness.
Did she toss that lick-shined wood
in the gutter? She holds her tongue
when, mixed with salt and heat, she senses
sugar in the greeting on his lips.

Although it was warm, and warm
was what she'd been missing.
Back to Madrona's safe peel
and smooth, its flesh of hers.
Leaf stubborn. Scars deep as roots,
lips of black-tailed deer.
Finches rise in the fields,
thistles gather without.
Porches with broken supports,
oranges too soft for morning.
Irises catch more light
than she thought coming.

SPAT

In unexpected rain the evening wash
swells along its hems, spills
in lazy drops. Braeburns gleam
like scarlet suns in mist,
on the balcony

no goldfinch comes. Bumblebees
strike the window, repeat
the tentative sound of rain.
The fence still holds
beneath the muscatels, skintight

clusters sheltered by green,
grape leaves dimpled with beads
slow on the leaf, the rail,
the pale blue towels
not drying on the line.

YEAR OF THE PLUM

That was the year she put up
sixty pints of butter from a single tree.
Persimmon-hued plums shaken to the ground,

gathered and washed, stewed and sieved,
simmered so low and long the steam
purpled her cheeks. That was the year

he won an altruism award from the fire district,
the year he cheated
to beat an eight-year-old at checkers.

That was the year the bedroom door
came off its hinges, the year of broken
wide-mouthed jars.

That was the year she hung
her shadow in the closet,
the year he took a chainsaw to the plum.

SOMETHING THERE IS

I will not accept the slow glint of stone
in your palm, evidence of something not
yours to give. You think you know the reason.
You don't know anything. What I mean is,
that cornered feeling that comes over you
comes over me and this, what you speak of
with a stone in your mouth, brings the walls in
close. I have lived most of my life closed in
by voices who only had in mind my
getting lost in their lives. Oh, I admit
my own desire to be lost in any
man who came along, but there's no mending
will fix this wall. The stones have disappeared.
I'll not open my fist to give them back.

SHE WAKES TO FIRE
Beneath J & K's outdoor shower, Indianola, Washington

not pine
not cottonwood
a tree she's never
tasted sweet and fierce
sunrise leaves her
fingers blazing yellow
sap rising and tears
with each breath the air
silent with her
smoldering

I ask the minister's modest wife to choose
the cake and flowers, pull a gown
from the clearance rack at Sears.
The minister's wife
wears band-aids on her nipples,
points out two frosted tiers, red roses.
The matron of honor, told to dress
as she pleased, also wears white,
because for her wedding
her mother insisted on ivory.
A silent walk in wet grass,
clouds bilious in a post-storm sky.
A calico cat creeps from the azalea,
stands between us, its tail
twitching through the vows.
The groom swears
to honor and cherish,
tosses me over his shoulder,
a gunnysack of apples, blood
draining from my face as he flips me
and drives me away.

THE SHADE GARDEN STAINED THE BRIDE'S DRESS
WITH IMPATIENS AND TOPSOIL

as she pulled herself through flowerbeds
below the picture window. Its hem caught
so many times on the heel of her sandal

that the borrowed ribbon stitched there
dragged behind and was stepped on
by the dog. When she climbed

the north side of the house, the green
mold of winter rubbed off the siding
and colored her hips. If we had bothered

to listen, we'd have heard chimney-rock
falling to the lawn, the catch of silk
on the window box, the scrape of her nails

against the wall. We should have recognized
the murmur of her dress
sweeping pine needles from the gutter

as she swung up to the roof. She sat there
on the peak with her skirts fanned out.
Grit from tarred shingles

worked its way into her skin. The gown
slipped from her shoulders. She peeled off
her undergarments, the last translucent slip,

the sun going down and the guests
chattering beneath her feet.

1.

Her 5th grade class watches the period film
and suddenly half of them are bleeding.
She tries to prove it with food coloring
but doesn't fool anyone. In her slam book
the boy she has a crush on can't spell:
blood not die, love Steve.

2.

She scoops ice cream and brews fresh Sumatran on the wharf.
Her apron is newly stained every day—
rainbow imprints on her breast from leaning into the freezer.

3.

In the Santa Barbara amphitheater
she sits on a cold stone
at Paul Simon's feet.
She has wanted inside that parka
for years. Late in the evening
she follows him home.

4.

In the girl's lavatory next to the music room, Kelly kisses her on the lips.
An unknown audience screeches out the door, lets in the sound of violins.

5.

He knocks her down for the last time.
She saves up, buys a trailer lousy with rodents.
She snaps their necks one after another,
turns her children loose in the woods to recover.

6.

Buddy delivers her first kiss. His lips are straw.
She hates him, but stares at his jeans when he's not looking.

7.

She births a boy
in 95 minutes with no help
and no noise.
When the doctor removes the baby's foreskin
without anesthetic,
she begins to cry;
she hasn't stopped since.

8.

The neighbor throws his wife against their common wall, screams
Give me some fucking head! A knock on the door
to see if the woman needs help. She says
she is fine. Swears at Frank and Gloria, the cats,
when they run out into the night between her legs.

9.

She falls from an alder and breaks her left arm, both bones
above the wrist. Her head hurts worse, but no one looks at it.

10.

David climbs on her in the back of his Dodge.
He is small but she doesn't know it.
She gives him back his ring, her hymen intact
until she meets a 30-year-old musician. He shows her
a picture of his 5-months pregnant girlfriend, taken a day before
the abortion. She flies to Seattle to rid herself of him.

11.

Her mother collapses with a bowl of pancake batter in her hands
and the morning sun gleaming off peppermint-oiled hardwood.
She is invited to sleep over at her girlfriend's almost every night.
There are never enough blankets.

12.

She bears another child, brushes her lips
across his lanugo before the nurse can dry him off.
Appendicitis keeps them apart overnight,
a separation from which neither recovers.

13.

She washes her Keds with Palmolive
and dries them on top of the heater.
The next day at recess when it is her turn,
her shoes slice through the puddle below the swing.
White foam bubbles into the water, each pass
frothing the little pond into a great lather,
but not so great that she can hide inside it.

RED SHRINE
Overlooking Admiralty Inlet, Port Townsend, Washington

Drape a sari in the Madrona
let its hem trail dry grass
pink silk and gold bead
seed pearls stitched into daisies
topaz thread in blossom
the sari touches earth
as the tree cradles
a slip of moon

Bark beneath a bolt of silk
what slips beneath skin
red curls away
the tender new
emerges and the sari
touches what is dead
yellow leaves
bits of twig and last year's fruit
above what is living

The Madrona sari
its silk like skin
beads like the song
we sang while washing
our hair in the bread bowl
with water we melted
from snow in deep winter
skin you shared with me
holding my hand
even when you did not want to

You are in the tree now
and I am in the cradle
I have not taken
money from your drawer
have not made fun of your thighs
nor left you behind
I have not failed
to recognize you there on the pavement
the sun a bright circle
of silk in your blood

Notes on the Poems

One Hundred Steps from Shore is dedicated to the memory of my sister, Carolyn.

Harbinger is for Roger and Hilary.

It was Snowing and It was Going to Snow: The title is taken from Wallace Steven's poem "Thirteen Ways of Looking at a Blackbird".

Porcupine Child is for Georgia.

Stephen's Passage Sonnet: The real name of the dog in the poem is Champion, our childhood companion, born not to hunt, but to fish.

She Stamps Her Feet is for Linda Browne.

Sweeping the Sky is dedicated to the memory of my father, Roger W. Browne, Jr.

Learning to Paint is for L.H.

Home Economics is for L.W.

Keeping Our Heads Underwater is for N.J.

Every Leap Year Dancing is for all the girls in junior high, then and now.

And We are Bound Away is in memory of M.C.

Something There Is borrows lines from "Mending Wall" and "Directive" by Robert Frost.

Tales from the 20th Century is for Judy.

Acknowledgments

I am grateful to the editors of the following publications, where these poems first appeared, sometimes in different form:

Art Access: Until Mother Finds Us Naked; You Can Smell the Rain Coming
Court Green: Stephen's Passage Sonnet
Exhibition: Year of the Plum
Kaleidowhirl: August Romance with Fruit Flies and Rot
North American Review: Vigils
Northwind: Learning to Paint
Potomac Review: Sweeping the Sky
Silk Road: Every Leap Year Dancing
Weathered Pages Anthology: Home Economics; Making Out; One Hundred Steps from Shore; Sticking to My Skin, Mica Moons Pull Me into the Current (under the title The Feeding Tide)
Windfall: A Cottonwood Leaf Can Be Taken Apart

My thanks and appreciation to the Centrum Foundation and Soapstone, for residencies that allowed me time to work on this manuscript, and to Artist Trust, for a grant that supported, in part, the creation of this work. Thanks also to Janet Knox and the West Port Madison poets for valuable insight and friendship in poetry. Kelli Russell Agodon has been a wellspring of advice and encouragement. I am grateful to Joseph Stroud, who provided a space for me to begin, and for the friendship of Dan Peters. Learning Dan's story helped me to tell this story. I am thankful for the generous spirit of Samuella Samaniego. Special thanks to Matt, for unflagging support and patience, and to Alex and Sam, whose stories need telling.

Cover panorama: "The Rain Keeper"
Frontispiece: "Dream Runners"

About the Author

Jenifer Browne Lawrence was born in California in 1958. Raised in Alaska, she currently lives in a small community near Seattle, Washington. Jenifer is the recipient of a Washington State Artist Trust grant and the *Potomac Review's* Annual Poetry Award. She has been a finalist for the James Hearst Poetry Prize. Her work has received a Pushcart nomination and is published in various journals and anthologies, including the *North American Review, The Comstock Review* and the *Potomac Review.*

About the Artist

Samuella Samaniego is an artist and assignment photographer of Native and Asian descent, born and raised in Southeast Alaska. Like so many other childhood friends, Jenifer and Sam became reacquainted via the great reach of the internet. Samuella is a well-traveled, award-winning, published and widely exhibited photographer who lives in Seattle with her partner and her dog.